Amelia Earhart

Terry Barber

FAMOUS FIRSTS SERIES

Amelia Earhart is published by
Grass Roots Press, a division of Literacy Services of Canada Ltd.

PHONE 1–888–303–3213
WEBSITE www.literacyservices.com

ACKNOWLEDGEMENTS

We acknowledge the financial support of the Government of Canada through the Book Publishing Industry Development Program (BPIDP) for our publishing activities.

We acknowledge the support of
the Alberta Foundation for the Arts
for our publishing programs.

 Alberta Foundation for the Arts

Editor: Dr. Pat Campbell
Image research: Dr. Pat Campbell
Book design: Lara Minja, Lime Design Inc.
Book layout: Andrée-Ann Thivierge, jellyfish design

Library and Archives Canada Cataloguing in Publication

Barber, Terry, date
        Amelia Earhart / Terry Barber.

(Famous Firsts series)
ISBN 978-1-894593-63-2

        1. Earhart, Amelia, 1897-1937. 2. Women air pilots--United States--Biography. 3. Readers for new literates. I. Title.

PE1126.N43B3639 2007   428.6'2   C2007-902783-0

Printed in Canada.

Contents

Amelia reads her scrapbook.

Heroes

Amelia keeps a scrapbook. She fills it with stories about women. These women are from all walks of life. They have one thing in common. They have jobs that men usually do. These women are Amelia's heroes.

Amelia Earhart, 1926.

Heroes

One day, Amelia will be a hero. She will be the first woman to fly across the Atlantic Ocean. Later, she will try to fly around the world. She does not return from this trip. Today, people still wonder what became of Amelia Earhart.

Amelia and Muriel play baseball.

Early Years

Amelia is born in Kansas on July 4, 1897. Amelia and her little sister Muriel are tomboys. They shoot rats. They climb trees. They play baseball. They keep worms, moths, and toads as pets.

Amelia Earhart, 1897.

A state fair in the early 1900s.

Early Years

When Amelia is ten, she goes to the state fair. She sees her first plane. Amelia shows no interest in the plane. She shows more interest in the merry-go-round. Ten years later, all she can think about is planes.

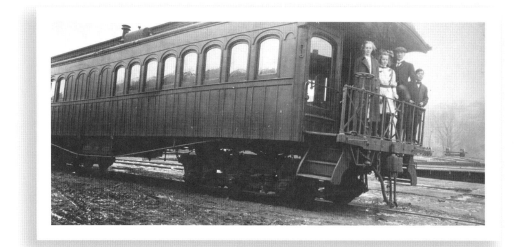

Amelia and her family move to another state.

Early Years

Amelia is happy as a child. Her teenage years are less happy. Her father moves from job to job. Her family moves from state to state. Amelia goes to many schools. She completes high school in 1916.

Amelia's family lives in Kansas, Minnesota, Illinois, and Iowa.

World War I lasts from 1914 to 1918.

Amelia is a nurse's aide during the war.

Early Years

Amelia goes to college. She drops out to work as a nurse's aide. The hospitals are filled with soldiers. These soldiers are hurt in World War I.

In 1919, Amelia goes back to school. She wants to be a doctor. Then her life changes.

Amelia Earhart, 1916.

Captain Frank Hawks takes Amelia on her first plane ride.

Amelia's Calling

Amelia finds her **calling** in 1920. She takes her first plane ride. The plane climbs. When it is about 300 feet (91 metres) off the ground, Amelia knows. Amelia knows she wants to be a pilot. She says, "I knew I had to fly."

Amelia finds her calling when she is 23 years old.

Neta Snook
teaches Amelia
how to fly.

Amelia Earhart and Neta Snook, 1921.

Amelia's Calling

Amelia takes flying lessons. She wants to own a plane. She saves money and buys a plane. She works odd jobs to pay for flying. In October 1922, Amelia sets a record. She is the first woman to fly to 14,000 feet (427 metres).

Amelia is a social worker.

Amelia's Calling

By 1924, Amelia runs into problems. Her health is not good. She has money problems. She cannot pay her bills. Amelia sells her plane. The next year, she moves to Boston. Amelia finds work as a teacher and a social worker.

Amelia is like a bird: they both need to fly.

The Atlantic Flight

In April 1928, Amelia gets a phone call. The caller asks, "Would you like to fly the Atlantic?" This is like asking a bird if it wants to fly.

Amelia says, "Yes." This flight will change her life.

Amelia returns to the U.S.

The Atlantic Flight

Amelia flies across the Atlantic Ocean. She flies with two men. The men pilot the plane.

The flight makes Amelia famous. She is the first woman to fly across the Atlantic. Amelia returns to the U.S. There is a parade in her honour.

President Herbert Hoover hosts a party for Amelia.

Amelia gives a speech.

The Celebrity

Amelia uses her fame to make a living. She promotes many products. She gives speeches. Amelia uses the money to keep flying.

Amelia races planes. She flies to 18,415 feet (5,613 metres). This is a new record for a woman.

In the 1920s, a female air race is called a "powder puff derby."

Amelia Earhart and George Putnam.

The Celebrity

Amelia marries a rich man in 1931.
Most women take their husband's last
name. Amelia keeps her last name. She
lives by her own rules. She lives life
her way.

Amelia Earhart marries George P. Putnam. Sometimes, he is called Mr. Earhart.

Many men think their wives should stay at home.

The Celebrity

Amelia believes men and women are equal. In the 1930s, many men do not share this belief. They think their wives should stay at home. Amelia does not stay at home. She keeps flying. She knows her husband supports her.

Amelia has **feminist** beliefs.

Amelia lands in Ireland after her solo flight.

The Celebrity

It is 1932. Amelia makes her mark as a pilot. She flies solo across the Atlantic. She is the first woman to make this trip alone. This trip makes her very famous. She gets many honours.

In 1935, Amelia flies **solo** from Hawaii to California. She is the first person to make this trip.

Amelia looks at a map of the world.

The Last Flight

Amelia is almost 40 years old. She sets a new goal. She wants to fly around the world. Amelia wants to follow the equator. She wants to "fly the world at its waistline."

Amelia and her navigator plan their trip.

The Last Flight

The trip is long and hard. Amelia
cannot fly alone. She needs a
navigator. This person will help
her stay on course. Amelia finds a
navigator. His name is Fred Noonan.

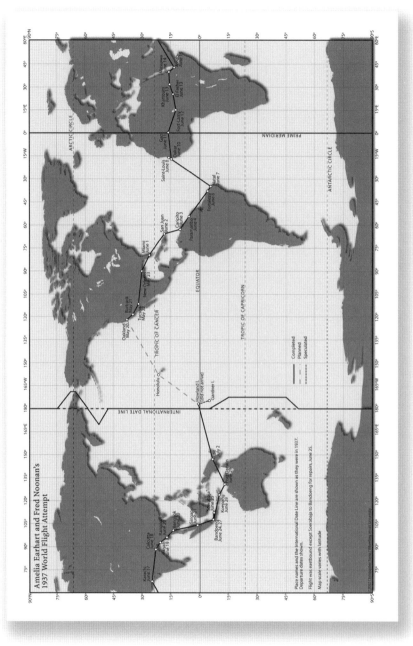

Amelia Earhart and Fred Noonan's
1937 World Flight Attempt

Amelia's route around the world.

The Last Flight

Amelia and Fred set out to make history. Their trip begins on June 1, 1937. The trip is about 29,000 miles (46,671 km). In the first month, they visit 19 countries. They travel 22,000 miles (35,406 km).

Amelia and Fred check the plane.

The last picture taken of Amelia and Fred, July 2, 1937.

The Last Flight

It is July 2, 1937. Amelia flies the longest leg of her trip. She flies over the Pacific Ocean. She must make one stop on a small island. Amelia cannot find the island. Her plane runs out of gas. Amelia is killed.

The longest **leg** is over 2,500 miles (4,023 km). It is from New Guinea to Howland Island.

Amelia makes the front page news.

The Last Flight

Or is Amelia killed? Some people say Amelia did not die. Some say she lived out her life on a Pacific island. Others say Amelia was a spy and the Japanese captured her. Nobody really knows what became of Amelia.

Amelia Earthart, 1932.

A Woman to Remember

People remember Amelia as a brave pilot. People remember her as a **role model.** Amelia said, "Fears are paper tigers." She said women "can act to change and control" their lives. This is how Amelia Earhart lived her life.

Glossary

calling: an inner urge to pursue an activity.

feminist: a person who believes that women and men should have equal rights and opportunities.

leg: part of a trip.

navigator: the person who figures out the position and course of an aircraft or ship.

role model: a person whose behaviour is copied by others.

solo: alone.